Thanks in part to the remote and rugged topography of Southwest China, the Dong people continue to display the richness of their cultural heritage as excellent musicians, superb architects, and makers of high quality textiles. Ancient structures such as 'wind and rain' bridges, are hallmarks of the Dong's unique culture. As in ages past, these bridges continue to grace the area's many rivers and streams, offering sheltered rest for weary travelers.

The village environment of the Dong is one of serene beauty, set beside meandering streams and wooded mountains. In the sheltered protection of these remote landscapes, age-old traditions have managed to survive, giving us an understanding of this little-known nationality.

This book is dedicated to the Dong people in the hope that their traditional customs and unique folk arts will continue to thrive during China's modernization drive.

Gail Rossi

AN ANCIENT PEOPLE

The remote mountain valley region where Guizhou, Guangxi and Hunan provinces meet constitutes the traditional homeland of China's Dong nationality. With a total population exceeding 1.4 million, 849,000 inhabit Guizhou, 318,000 live in Hunan and 229,000 in Guangxi. Dong communities living in different areas vary considerably in both customs and traditional clothing styles. At least 30 distinct dress groups can be found among the Dong; seldom do Dong from one dress style marry into a Dong group of a differing style. Generally, the Dong nationality can be divided into "Northern" and "Southern" Dong. Dong from the northern counties of Guizhou's Tianzhu, Jinping, Sansui and Jianhe have lost many traditions due to stronger Han influence, as these areas are in close proximity to a main transportation route. Dong in the more remote southern areas of Guizhou, and in Hunan and Guangxi have retained their diverse culture, traditional dress styles, and unique architecture.

The Dong language belongs to the Zhuang-Dong branch of the Sino-Tibetan language family. The language of the Dong is similar to the Shui, Dai, Zhuang, Buyi, Maonan, and Gelao languages. There are basically two dialects, "northern" and "southern", with each containing 3 sub-dialects. The northern dialect includes Dong living in Jianhe, Sansui, and Jinping counties of Guizhou. The southern dialect can be found in Liping, Rongjiang, Congjiang, Tongdao, Longshu, Sanjiang, Zhenyuan, Rongshui and southern Jinping of Guizhou, Hunan and Guangxi provinces.

Reference to the Dong nationality can be found in ancient Chinese historical sources from as far back as the Qin Dynasty (221-207 B.C.) where they were referred to as "Qian Zhong Man". During the Han Dynasty (206 B.C. - 220 A.D.) they were known as "Wuximan" or "Wulingman" which included several other nationalities. In the Northern and Southern Dynasties (420-589 A.D.) the Dong were called the "Liao" people.

In the Song Dynasty (960-1279 A.D.) they were designated variously as "Ge-ling", "Ge-Lao", "Ge-lan", "Ge-lou", "Miao", "Yao", etc.

Plum blossoms through early morning mist in Zhenyuan's Baojing village, Guizhou.

Laughing girl from Tongle Village in Sanjiang County of Guangxi.

In the Ming Dynasty (1368-1644 A.D.) they were known as "Dong" with a "Shan" radical. In the Qing (1644-1911 A.D.), they were variously termed "Dong Miao", "Dong Min", "Dong Jia" or simply "Miao".

The Dong call themselves "Gan",("gaeml" in Dong language), "Geng" ("geml") or "Jin" ("jeml"). Also they call themselves "Jin lao" ("jeml laox"), "Jin jiao" ("jeml jaox"), and "Jin tan" ("jeml tanx").

The Dong are believed to have originated from a branch of the ancient "Luo Yue" people, and are known to have lived in Guizhou during the end of the Eastern Han Dynasty (206-B.C.-220 A.D.). The "Luo Yue" were native people of the area now inhabited by the Dong. Through time, the ancient "Ba Yue" people migrated into this same region, mingling with the native population. The Dong are thought to have derived from these people.

In everyday life, there exists among the Dong, animistic religious beliefs and practices; benevolent and malevolent spirits exist everywhere in nature. Valleys, rivers, mountains, trees and rocks, the netherworld, bridges and wells, all have spiritual significance and attending spirits that must be acknowledged and taken care of in the proper way, so as to not destroy an existing balance. In some parts of the mountains, the land cannot be dug; some trees are not to be cut; there are stones that cannot be cracked. If people trespass against these beliefs, it is believed disaster is sure to follow.

A procession of villagers during the "Huapao" (Fireworks) festival in Guangxi, delivers a winning trophy—mirror with red cloth—to the home of the lucky winner, who may keep the prize for one year. Men playing lusheng music lead the way, followed by a line of people dressed in various disguises, adding to the fun.

Above: A mother and daughter from Shuangjiang Village, Liping County, Guizhou.

Below: Young man in traditional dress, joins a procession during a festive occasion in Sanjiang, Guangxi; he carries his hunting rifle, decorated with auspicious green leaves and loaded with firecrackers to set off along the way.

Right: During New Year celebrations held in Chengyang Village in Sanjiang, lion dances amuse the village crowds. Below: Dong women, especially from the south, wear traditional costume every day of the year; the best are worn for festivals.

Young woman from Sanjiang refills a gun with gun powder from the gourd she carries, during New Year celebrations.

Dong homes, generally made of China Fir, are two to four story dwellings. In most areas, the upper floors serve as living quarters, while the lower floor is kept for domestic animals and storage. The front central half of the home upstairs, containing an open fireplace, is the center of activity in a Dong house; this room is traditionally open and spacious for family reunions and for daily workspace where the women weave and spin, men make fish nets and baskets, young children play, and where old folks rest and chat.

The elderly are provided with heated bedrooms in the back part of the house, while the rest of the family have bedrooms off the main part of the home. Ten to twelve rooms, according to a family's economic situation, is about average. In other Dong areas, such as Tianzhu and Rongjiang, the family live downstairs, and the second floor is used for storage; animals then live in rooms to the sides of the home.

Finely carved wooden porches, covered for protection from sun and rain, are another common feature of Dong homes, used as a center for family activity during warm weather. Looms and spinning wheels generally find their place on the porch. Washed clothing and long lengths of brilliantly dyed cloth are hung from porch rafters. Damp pleated skirts are often affixed to a porch beam, carefully tied to keep the tiny pleats in place after washing.

Preceding page: Ancient traditions and modernization have so far managed to harmoniously exist side by side in Dong communities such as in Zhaoshing, of Liping County in Guizhou. Homes with electricity, paved roads and a new modern school building have made their appearance in recent years. Over 700 families inhabit Zhaoshing, the largest Dong village in China.

Above: Young boy gives his dog a bath in the Fulu River in Sanjiang; his family's boat is used not only for fishing but also for transport.

Left: An older Dong man and his hunting gun are inseparable, even while shopping in a department store, in Fulu.

Left: Everywhere men and women carry items on shoulder poles, whether working in the fields, going to market, visiting friends or doing housework. This man from Shuikou, Liping, uses his hunting rifle as a shoulder pole. The woman is from Fulu, Sanjiang.

Below: Most Dong men are heavy smokers. The tobacco is home-grown in most villages. Cigarettes are rolled by hand and smoked in crude ceramic pipes.

Above: Young women in Baojing, Zhenyuan wear commercially made towels around their heads, a practice now commonly widespread among many ethnic groups of China's southwest. Every year on the third day of the third lunar month, the Baojing Dong hold their traditional spring sowing festival, which also provides the young with courting opportunities. The day before, all young women net fish from the village's rice paddies, which are then presented to young men. Together they roast the fish. Later the entire village, young and old, join in on the feasting.

Right: An older woman from Baojing (a Dong village of over 1000 people) continues to wear the traditional handloomed turban.

DAILY LIFE

Above: A woman and her daughter pick fresh vegetables from their back-yard garden, in Baojing, Zhenyuan.

Below: The inside walls of the main room in most Dong homes proudly exhibit various certificates and other prizes awarded members of their family, such as this "Literacy Certificate". Illiteracy is still a problem to be resolved in remote villages.

Music and song are an important and ever-present aspect of the Dong's culture. People often sing while working the fields and as they do housework; at funerals they sing in grief, while at birthdays and weddings they sing for fun. According to Dong traditions, important guests must be greeted by songs before they can cross the threshhold of a home and as they depart. But the musical nature of the Dong really come to flower on festive occasions.

The Dong are especially famous for their chorus singing, where men and women sing different tunes in turn. Many evenings, there are get-togethers in village drum towers where polyphonic singing accompanies the music of pipas and special ox-legged shaped Dong guitars.

Dong choruses imitate sounds from nature. Birds, insects, and murmuring brooks, have long inspired the people inhabiting these remote regions.

Traditionally the Dong had no written form of their language. Instead, the Dong's history and ancient legends were imbedded in song which have been passed down through the ages. During important festivals, such songs are always sung to the young.

Preceding page: Children from Baojing are dressed in their finest for the "Qing Ming" (Pure Bright) Festival. Graffiti is a common sight on wooden walls of village buildings, a place where children practice writing in chalk, the characters they learn in school.
Opposite: Video Cinemas have grown so much in popularity they are now even found in remote areas. Instead of buying a ticket, these women line up to take a peek from outside.

Woman from Fulu, Sanjiang, transports sheaves of glutinous rice from the field to her home.

While caring for young children, women gather together to do embroidery, sewing and to catch up on the latest village talk.

Above: One of the daily chores for a woman is to gather floating duckweed from flooded rice-paddies to feed the family pig; she likewise catches a few fish grown in the rice-paddies for dinner, which are brought home in a hanging bamboo basket.

Left: Dong women are allowed to have two children according to law. In one remote village in Congjiang County, the women have for centuries practiced this limit out of tradition by partaking of a mountain herb after the second birth, preventing further pregnancies.

Left: Wooden statues sit inside the altar in the middle of the covered bridge in Baxie, Sanjiang.

Right: A fire prevention plaque on the doorway of a Dong home, exhorts villagers to be careful, while the religious symbol below, offers spiritual protection for the household. In some villages, the fire spirit is paid homage to by sacrificing a pig.

Above: A small temple set midway in a covered bridge in Baxie, Sanjiang, gives villagers and passersby the chance to remember their ancestors and provides the opportunity to petition for spiritual help in worldly matters.

Dong woman from Chenyang, Sanjiang.

Young people generally marry at the age of 17 or 18. Throughout Dong history, the young were free to choose marriage partners of their choice, through singing competitions and other activities held especially during festivals. In the past 10 years, arranged marriages have become more common. Elopement also occurs, after which the boy must ask one of his relatives to visit the girl's family to apologize. A date is set to kill a pig; the young man then delivers it to the girl's family, thus "washing his face" of any impropriety.

If the sentiment is strong between an introduced couple, the boy will ask a close relative to go to the girl's home to propose marriage. If consent is given, discussion follows to negotiate the date of marriage. In some areas people consult geomancers to calculate the safest and most promising wedding day. In other places, a chicken is killed to determine whether the marriage will be good or not, according to the open or closed eyes of the dead chicken. If the answer is negative, some couples will break off the engagement.

After the date has been set, the boy's family will bring gifts to the girl's family such as ducks, fish, silver or gold. In return, the girl's family give gifts of cloth and embroidered shoe liners. The boy's family continues giving gifts to the girl's family until pregnancy occurs.

The last step in marriage is the ceremony itself which is celebrated in different ways according to region. Generally the bride is fetched by a relative of the husband, accompanied by the bride's good friends. Family and friends are entertained with food, wine and singing. In many areas, it is forbidden for the bride's family members to enter the groom's village during the first day's wedding celebrations.

Dong couples generally will not live together as man and wife directly after the wedding. The girl returns to her village and only during festivals, or heavy farming seasons, will she come to spend the night with her husband. After pregnancy occurs she will finally move into her husband's home.

Both husband and wife can divorce only if they first consult the village elders and after their families try their best to convince the couple to remain together. The person who desired the divorce must pay living expenses for the other partner. Children will be raised by both parents.

Left: Villagers visit the dentist during market days where service is rendered outdoors. This particular dentist came especially for the annual festival in Shuangjiang, Liping. Preventative dentistry is virtually unknown. A visit is necessary when pain persists.

Left: Historically the Dong people had no written language until one was developed in 1956. Today, Dong children in some county schools are taught to write in both the Han and Dong language, especially in the south.

Above: Young Dong girls play a game with coins in Baojing.
Below: For easier care, young children's heads, especially boys, are often partially or entirely shaven.

Bamboo bobbins, used for winding weaving threads, are sold in abundance at the market during the "Sanyuesan" festival in Fulu, Sanjiang.

Right: Every household has its musket-loading hunting gun propped in its appointed place within the home, alongside powder horns. Following ancient custom, a hunter always shares his kill with whoever accompanies him hunting. During the hunting season, the men will first pay their respects to the mountain spirit before the hunt, to ensure good luck and safety.

Below: Dong men enjoy the melodic singing of song birds which they keep in finely carved cages. Many hours are spent training birds to improve their singing. Ox fights and bird fights are another activity enjoyed by the men during festivals.

Above: Long narrow boats are the main mode of transport for villagers living along the Duliu river flowing through Fulu. During weekly markets, the "taxi" boats are filled to capacity.

Below: A group of Dong women watch an outdoor opera show in Baxie, Sanjiang.

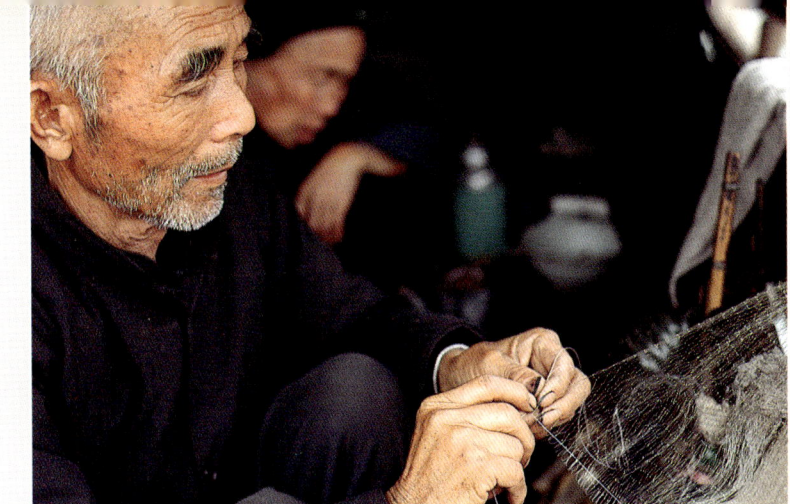

Right: Mending a fishing net, in Fulu, Sanjiang.

Below: Dong prefer to build their villages alongside meandering streams, where women can clean their clothing, prepare for indigo dyeing, wash vegetables, and where ducks and children can play.

Above: A stream of people carry items from their villages, miles away, to sell at the annual "Sanyuesan" market held in Fulu, Sanjiang.

Right: Wooden masts surround a temple in Zhaoxing, Liping, representing thanks to the gods for delivering a male son. Before the Cultural Revolution (1966-1977), the vast number of standing masts resembled a forest.

During the "Qing Ming" festival in Baojing, Zhenyuan, the Dong people show respect to their dead ancestors by cleaning the grave sites, and by bringing along a feast to eat beside the graves of their loved ones. Not a time of sorrow, it is a joyous occasion. Food is first offered to their ancestors.

FARMING AND FOOD

Since ancient times, the Dong people have traditionally dwelt in mountain river valleys where, with the help of water buffaloes, they practice rice cultivation in irrigated fields and along steep mountain terraces. The men are expected to sow the fields, do heavy farmwork and other labor, while the women spend much time weaving, doing housework and light gardening. During busy farm seasons the women will join in sowing and harvesting grains. In a very few districts, women do all the heavy fieldwork, while the men stay home to look after the children and do housework.

Fish ponds are scattered throughout a village. Grain is often stored on racks over these ponds, to protect precious staples against possible fire damage and as a deterrent to rats. Fish are likewise raised in flooded rice paddies.

Left: In Guizhou, Guanxi and Hunan, fields of blossoming rape are found throughout the rural areas from as early as February. The seeds are pressed for their oil, which is used for cooking and other purposes.

Above: Assorted vegetable greens, used to make sour vegetable soup, are chopped and sun dried on roof tops.

Above: Threshing rice is a common activity in autumn, a job usually practiced by women as in this household in Shuangjiang, Liping.

Below: Women spend much time in the fields transplanting rice seedlings.

Woman collects duckweed floating on a flooded rice field to use as pig's feed.

Right: It is always the men's job to plow the rice fields using the help of water buffalo.

Below: A man draws water from a pool into the fields with a simple manual pump. On high mountain terraces, any spare space is used to store rain water in pools and to raise fish at the same time.

"Nuo mi" (glutinous rice) is the staple food among the Dong. In the autumn, southern Dong villages, such as in Congjiang county, are transformed to a mellow color of gold as rows and rows of towering drying racks are hung with harvested sheaves of glutinous rice. Because of its stickiness, glutinous rice can be conveniently eaten by hand, without chopsticks.

When Dong go off to the fields and mountains to work, or travel long distances on foot, they will always wear attached to their belt, a small round covered basket filled with glutinous rice. In a smaller wooden container, also tied to their belt, is a ready supply of salty hot sauce, made of smoked or pickled peppers, to accompany the rice.

Opposite: Because of mountainous terrain, terraces must be cut; rice paddies are then formed along steep inclines.

Below: Transplanting new rice seedlings in Baojing, Zhenyuan. Wherever level land is available, there is intense cultivation.

Fields are often miles from home. Family members pack a lunch and walk far distances to do required work before returning home in late afternoons. Young children spend the time playing while older siblings learn to do farmwork.

On occasions like weddings, funerals and other celebrations, the most appropriate presents to give are two baskets of glutinous rice. In some areas, such as Liping, cooked glutinous rice is dyed a blue-green and given as a wedding gift. The Dong in Rongjiang and other counties prepare a special "black-rice", dyed from the leaves of a certain tree, for a festival known as "Eat Black Rice".

For special events, glutinous rice is beaten to a paste in heavy wooden or stone containers. Family members take turns with the heavy pounding. Known locally as "baba", the resultant paste is formed into round patties. After drying, they become hard as rocks and can be stored for several months if placed in a bucket of cool water, changing the water daily. Before eating, a patty is placed on red coals until it softens, becoming bubbly and golden in color. One small cake is equivalent to several bowls of rice.

The first floor of a Dong's kitchen is filled with sweet fragrance as wooden barrels of rice wine are brewing. During weddings, festivals, when guests visit and for other important occasions, an abundance of wine is drunk with meals. Wine is also given as offerings to various nature spirits and to ancestors on prescribed occasions.

Dong are renowned for their spicy cured fish. Fish raised in rice-paddy fields are coated with salt and hot pepper, and kept in clay containers for several years; the resultant spicy, salty and sour fish is eaten cold or hot during festivals, weddings and when special guests arrive. Raw, pickled pork is another favorite food served at wedding celebrations.

Right: Vegetables are extensively cultivated near village homes in Fulu, Guangxi. Villages are surrounded by China Fir, tea oil and tung oil trees. Care is taken to protect certain ancient trees in each village, as they are considered sacred. It is believed that the tree's spirit will ensure the village's peace and safety.

Below: Women prepare vegetables for drying, which later will be made into preserved vegetables, a salty sour concoction savored by the Dong people as an accompaniment to rice.

Right: Guests visiting a Dong home in Guangxi will be invited to partake in oiled tea. In a pot hanging above the main room's fire pit, the woman of the house will pour a little tea oil, dried puffed glutinous rice, soybeans and peanuts. After stirring awhile, she places this mixture into each tea bowl. Tea leaves known as "mist tea", are then placed in the pot, and hot water is added. When boiled, this is poured into each bowl. According to custom, each guest should drink three bowls of such tea. It is believed to help aid digestion, treat colds and to increase mental activity.

Below: (1) Dyed and undyed glutinous rice is mixed together and placed in baskets for carrying on distant trips to markets or to other villages.
(2) The ingredients for "oil tea": fried rice, peanuts, soy beans and different kinds of fried "baba" (glutinous rice cakes). Dried tea leaves lie underneath.
(3) Glutinous rice is dyed yellow (and other colors) on special occasions. The herb next to the basket is immersed in water; rice is soaked in the resulting yellow dye liquid for several hours, and then steamed.

Left: A grandmother from Chengyang forms round cakes of "baba" which are eaten either plain, dipped in sugar, or filled with cooked beans.

Below: Women from Tongle, Sanjiang, beat dried glutinous rice to a flour.

Left: After beating glutinous rice in a stone urn with a wooden mallet, a mother presents a string of the sticky "baba" to her child.

Right: A family in Tongle, Sanjiang, prepares "oil tea" for friends who have come to visit.

Below: A group of young people stop for a picnic lunch on their way to a distant market, in Fulu, Sanjiang. Such lunches commonly consist of glutinous rice, sticks of cooked pork, preserved sour vegetables and hot sauce.

FESTIVALS

Dong festivals occur throughout each year, providing opportunities for young men and women to meet one another, and for friends and relatives to be reunited. Various activities are held such as singing contests, dances, music, plays, ox and bird fights and sometimes religious ceremonies.

Participating in festive activities are traditional steps for young people towards courtship and marriage. According to custom, several weeks before an important festival, village elders send their young men to several nearby villages to invite the unmarried girls to attend.

On the eve of the festival, the young men come to the village of the invited women with flutes and drums, and bring them back to gather in their village's drum tower. After a rich feast, the young men and women sit in parallel rows facing one another under the eyes of their elders and get to know one another by spontaneously singing to each other. Until dawn, traditional songs mingle with the playing of flutes and stringed instruments.

Festivals offer important courtship opportunities for young men and women.

The next morning, dressed in their finest woven and embroidered clothing, and adorned with handmade silver bangles, the women meet together in their own village drum tower to wait. From the other village, the young men deliberately walk back and forth three times playing flutes and drums before the women are "coaxed" into accompanying them to their village for more festivities.

At festivals such as during the lunar New Year, an open fire is lit at the site of the festive feast. In the first circle around the fire sit the village elders and invited guests; next, a circle of women, and then a circle of young men. The mother of each girl sits nearby. A contest proceeds, when male and female singers pair off. The themes of the songs express love and beauty, heavily veiled in metaphors and subtle allusions. The male singer starts the improvisation and the woman responds.

This is a competition to not only test the singing voices of the couples, but also their cleverness in simultaneously improvising new words to old songs. The atmosphere is charged with teasing, claps and cheers. Later, the entire village joins in and sings traditional songs.

Below: The bamboo reed instrument, known as "lusheng" is a popular musical instrument among the Dong. Large lushengs are used mainly on festive occasions, to accompany group dances. Smaller ones are used not only for making music for general enjoyment, but also for courting.

Left: The Han Chinese have had a certain amount of influence among Dong living in Guangxi; lion dances as a form of entertainment are one aspect of Han Chinese culture borrowed by the Dong.

Right: Dong women in Fulu, stand in groups to observe the games held during the Fireworks Festival.

Below: In Baojing, Zhenyuan, the neighbouring Miao bring along their drums to join the Dong for Sanyuesan festivities.

During the Lunar New Year in Sanjiang, Liping and Congjiang counties, the Dong hold commemorative activities to honor their "Grandmother". A procession of young men and women (see above) carry hunting rifles to mimic going off to battle, in memory of a Dong heroine, Xing Ni, who died for the Dong's freedom over 1000 years ago. Known as "Sasui" (Grandmother in Dong language), many villages have erected temples in her honor.

The young people stop along the way to fire off shots, and let off firecrackers. Small iron cannons placed in the fields are likewise set off, creating a cacophony of noise (right). Men carry flags and guns decorated with leaves and paper streamers. Each village has its own unique form of decoration.

Late in the day a feast is held for the young people. The young men bring out skewers of grilled pork (a symbol of union) and glutinous rice cakes to give as gifts to the women. They then escort the women home.

Upon reaching the women's village, couples can be alone with one another at an appointed spot near the girl's home. There they will sing love songs to one another and share the food given.

Above: As firecrackers resound, part of the New Year procession wear old Chinese costumes in jest, followed behind by lion dancers, and lusheng players.

Below: Newly arrived visitors are welcomed by villagers with songs of greeting.

Next page: Thousands of people of several nationalities line the river bank of the Duliu in Fulu, Sanjiang during the Fireworks Festival to attend the important market and to join in on festive activities.

The Sanyuesan Festival

On the third day of the third lunar month of every year, the Dong in Sanjiang celebrate the Fireworks Festival, also known as "Sanyuesan". While this festival is also observed in several Dong areas on the first and second lunar months, the largest celebration is held in a town called Fulu in Sanjiang County, Guangxi Province. Dong, Miao and Yao nationalities attend this yearly event, each dressed in their respective festive dress. Peasants and peddlers line the streets and riverbank with their wares, providing a wide range of products: weaving and spinning equipment, silk threads, furniture, clothing, tools and appliances.

The Fireworks Festival has been celebrated in Fulu town for over one hundred years. Competitive activities dominate this festival, abounding in explosions of firecrackers. "Grabbing the Hoop" is the most popular game. Thousands of people form a ring around a bonfire, awaiting the arrival of young men carrying the "huapao" — three metal hoops that are individually wrapped in red cloth and placed on top of three long cylinders containing explosives. They are led by a procession of musicians, and followed by carriers of prizes. When lit, these three huge firecrackers carry the hoops skyhigh. As it descends, a hundred or more young men grab for the ring. This activity is played three times, once for each ring. The first ring stands for wealth and long life, the second for promotions and the third for fertility. The lucky winners are awarded colorfully decorated trophies, called "pao-ping" which are filled with meat, money and rice wine, and are decorated with paper figures, horses, houses, flowers and a mirror. The responsibility of providing the awards and firecrackers for the next festival falls on the winners.

The gaiety and color of the festival draw capacity crowds from neighbouring communities. Below are the trophies for winners of the game.

A procession of musicians blowing lushengs and suona horns (a wood-wind instrument) lines the riverbank in the late afternoon, loaded with firecrackers, paper-flowers and awards. As the winners accept their trophies, a deafening blast of firecrackers, gongs, drums and suona horns fills the region.

In the evening, people return to their villages. Local Dong operas are performed, and sometimes a film is shown, while a lusheng party is held under a huge banyan tree. Families entertain each other with wine and good food, especially guests who have come from far places. Throughout the night the young people sit around firepits, singing and plucking tunes on their pipas (a stringed instrument). Activities of this festival not only offer courtship opportunities for the young, but also give the entire community a momentary escape from life's everyday toil.

Above: Outdoor operatic play held during the New Year in Baxie, Sanjiang.

Below: Opera in Tongle.

The Dong people are renowned for their folk drama. Their literary history is abundant with narrative poems, pipa songs and epics.

A man named Wu Wencai wrote and performed the first Dong operatic play, "Mei Liangyu", about 150 years ago. Accompanied by lyric pipa songs, this play marked the formation of a Dong tradition that is still being carried out today.

Stories of Dong plays come from both Han and Dong narrative poems. Some are historical plays, such as "Wu Mian", a hero from the Ming Dynasty who led 200,000 Dong and Miao people in a series of uprisings covering a period of eight years. In the play, Wu Mian takes on mythical properties.

Although drawn from Han theatrics, Dong drama has its own unique characteristics, such as the inclusion of a clown, a figure often depicted to delight and amuse the audience.

The clowns wear black masks or paint white lines on their faces and noses. Some paint a frog on their noses or the Chinese character symbolizing "good luck" and "good harvest".

Almost every village has amateur opera troupes, who are often invited to perform in neighboring villages, towns and cities where they are warmly received by young and old. They are greeted with good-hearted jests and songs of greeting by villagers and townfolk who block their way by putting obstacles in their entry path. The villagers allow them to pass only after the actors reply in song.

Above: Dressing in costume for Dong opera.

Below: Men from Chengyang wearing silver necklets, apply make-up in a humorous manner for the New Year festivities.

DRESS

Evidence of a flourishing textile tradition is apparent most everywhere in southern Dong areas. Time-honored traditions of weaving, spinning and dyeing continue to thrive. Long narrow strips of indigo-dyed cloth dry on stony river banks or flat grass fields after soaking the fabric in wooden tubs of pig's blood. Mothers walking to market carry their children in finely embroidered or woven baby carriers of harmonious design. Yards of handwoven fabric, hung out and shimmering brilliantly after a long dyeing process, billow from a two-story porch of a Dong home. The reverberating sound of dyed cloth being patiently beaten on flat stones by the women becomes everyday "music" drifting through southern Dong villages.

Because of the southwest's geographical isolation, the Dong nationality living in remote river valleys have had little contact with outside groups. Mountainous seclusion has helped preserve the ancient modes of dress which have remained virtually unchanged for hundreds of years.

Today, with the advent of better transportation, such isolated areas are gradually being opened to the outside world, resulting in costume alterations. Now, available time savers such as machine-produced braid and synthetic cloth, are frequently incorporated into the customary dress. Young girls in some areas have abandoned time-consuming embroidery details learned from their mothers in favor of simplified designs of brighter colors.

Above: Woman from Zhaoxing, Fulu wears plastic flowers in her hair.

Opposite: Festive costumes from Fulu include handmade cloth shoes, embellished with embroidery.

Above: Woman from Fulu.

Right: During the winter months, women wear padded clothing and dress in several layers of garments to keep out the cold.

Courting festivals, rich in polyphonic singing and simple dances, offer occasions for young Dong women to dress in their finest handwoven, dyed, and embroidered clothing, ornamented with an abundance of silver jewelry that jangles musically on their festive aprons.

On such occasions, an unmarried woman presents a special handwoven bag or vest to the young man she most favors. The young man, if he in turn admires the woman, will sing spontaneous praises of her skillfullness at the loom. A person's ability to sing is equally praised among the Dong, and is another important factor in the selection of a mate.

Above: A Miao woman, second from front, joins in on a Dong dance during the "Sanyuesan" festival in Zhenyuan.

Right: Women from Congjiang wear costumes dyed in indigo, pig's blood and egg whites.

Above: Under-apron and jacket front decorations are a combination of patterned weaving and satin-stitch embroidery done in silk. This dress style comes from Tongle, in Sanjiang and differentiates the wearer from other Dong dress groups of other areas. It is worn for festivals.

Right: Baby carriers worn by Dong women from Fulu are elaborately embroidered and ornamented with small mirrors, a style found among Dong also in parts of southern Guizhou, and a few Miao nationality dress groups.

Right: Women wear embroidered sashes in Fulu, hung to both sides of their waist. The Chinese character "ping", meaning "peace", is embroidered on both ends. Various characters are commonly integrated in clothing decoration, not only for its pleasing form, but also for its meaning.

Below: Another variation of costume from Tongle.

Section of woven and embroidered jacket sleeve.

The making of traditional costumes continues to play an important role in a woman's life. Each Dong dress group has its own traditions and produces distinct clothing that reflects its particular customs, history and beliefs. Cultural identity is thus maintained through the making and wearing of such garments.

Festivals and especially market days reveal the wide array of dress differences found among the Dong people. Much can be gleaned from one glance at a woman's costume as to not only where she comes from, but also how diligent she is as a worker and how creative an artist. For this reason, young women continue to learn from their mothers and grandmothers the technical intricacies of weaving long-cherished patterns into their cloth, the tedious hours of dyeing fabric to perfection, the ability to spin a fine thread and the patient skill needed to elaborately embroider garments. In some Dong areas, years of labor go into the making of one complete festive and marriage costume.

Another factor is responsible for the preservation of ancient textile techniques, styles and motifs — a woman's chances of marriage are closely aligned to her textile skills. One of the criteria a Dong man looks for in a prospective wife is her proficiency in embroidery, dyeing and weaving. A young girl begins learning the textile arts at the age of seven or eight, so by the time she reaches marriageable age, she'll have prepared one or more sets of festive clothing, painstakingly created to show her ability. The countless hours of needlework are exhibited during the many courting festivals held throughout the year, when women parade their most exquisite handmade costumes in the hope of attracting a desirable young man.

Left: A woman wears her family's wealth in the form of silver jewelry during festive occasions, in the hope of attracting a future spouse. A man and woman introduce themselves to each other by singing about their lives. Gradually, if the attraction deepens, the two will sing love songs to one another.

Right: A woman from Baojing, Zhenyuan wears her finest embroidered garments and ample silver jewelry during both weddings and festivals.

Below: Heavy silver chains are worn by women from Baojing during festive occasions.

Above: During market day, women in some areas wear simple back carriers for carrying their market purchases.

Below: Babies and young children wear hats richly decorated with silver figurines and bangles not only during festive occasions but also on market and visiting days.

In the south, both festive and everyday wear are woven from cotton grown in nearby fields. The spinning wheel, an indispensible item of a woman's dowry, is found on the spacious wooden porch of the Dong's sturdy fir house, where women gather together to spin smooth cotton and linen threads. Eventually, the cloth they weave will be transformed, through dyeing, into a unique iridescent fabric.

From the age of 13, Dong women working on floor looms produce yards of plain-woven cloth to be used in traditional clothing. The Dong are famous for their colorful brocade weavings that are incorporated into aprons, shoulder bags, baby-carriers and household items. The most common brocade motifs are camelias, human figures, animals and geometric patterns. Both floor looms and small belt looms are used to weave narrow bands of simple yet beautiful designs for straps and apron ties. In Guizhou's Congjiang and Liping counties, women weave delicate designs on low foot-pull body-tension looms containing over 300 supplemental harness sticks.

Jackets, trousers, leggings, finely pleated skirts, backless under-aprons and baby carriers are traditionally made from any one of three basic-dyed fabrics: an almost black indigo-dyed cloth; a stiff reddish-purple cloth, dyed first in indigo, then pounded with a mixture of cow's hide and blood; and a fabric dyed with the previous method, yet further coated with a mixture of egg whites, producing a lasting high-gloss sheen.

Opposite: Dong girl from Fulu, dressed for market, holds her shoulder pole.

It is in the remote south where needlework of exquisite beauty, workmanship and variety can be found among the Dong people.

On sweltering summer days, Dong women (some as young as seven) sit on low stools set in mountain brooks under the shade of roofed "wind and rain" bridges, embroidering intricate designs on strips of white cloth — handwoven from threads finely spun from cotton grown in nearby fields. Any spare moment is caught to add a few more inches to their embroidered edgings and squares used to decorate bags (worn at the waist), baby carriers, apron yokes and jacket sleeves.

A favorite embroidery technique among the Dong of Liping, is a simple counted straight stitch which requires great skill in creating the precise tiny patterns they so cherish. Eighty stitches to an inch is not uncommon.

The beating of working looms is an ever-present rhythm found in Dong villages. Dong weaving is reputed for its fine quality of homespun cotton threads and intricate brocade designs. Bed coverings, baby carriers and bags are embellished with such fine weavings. Numerous folk stories relate the mythical origins of Dong weaving.

SPINNING, WARP PREPARATION AND WEAVING

1. A rolag is made by beating a cotton boll. The seeds from the boll are removed by placing through the rollers of a wooden cotton gin. After spinning, the cotton is wound on a bamboo stick on the end of the spindle of a spinning wheel. **2**. A woman spins on a bamboo spinning wheel, winding the spun thread onto a bobbin. **3**. Another kind of spinning wheel. Rolags sit in basket and spun threads are wrapped on the bobbin. **4**. Bobbin holder in foreground. The yarn is measured on a unique type of niddy noddy in preparation for measuring warp for the loom. **5**. Wetting cotton to set the twist and to shrink the fibers before weaving. The woman is wringing out the skein of cotton by the method of twisting using a stick. **6**. Pulling on cotton skein prior to putting it on the reel which will help separate the fibers. **7**. Drawing the thread from the reel to the thick bamboo spools which will be set up for warping.

8. Threads are strengthened by wax application. 9. Warping on a horizontal warping board using multiple threads from the bamboo spools. 10. Lease sticks are placed in the warp, and warp threads are spaced in the bamboo reed. 11. One woman rolls up the warp on warp rod, while the other separates threads by beating them with her hand and moving the reed up and down. 12. Finally, after the warp is attached to the loom, a woman can begin weaving. Here she weaves on a low foot-pull loom, a forerunner of the looms used later in Korea, Okinawa and Japan. 13. Woman weaving cloth on a counterbalance loom. 14. After woven cloth has been dyed, a woman spends hours beating the cloth to enhance sheen and to strengthen the fibers.

Dong women wear their long hair tied up in assorted knots and buns, which are further adorned with a wide variety of silver chains, combs, flowers and pins, in the style reflecting their ancestral tradition.

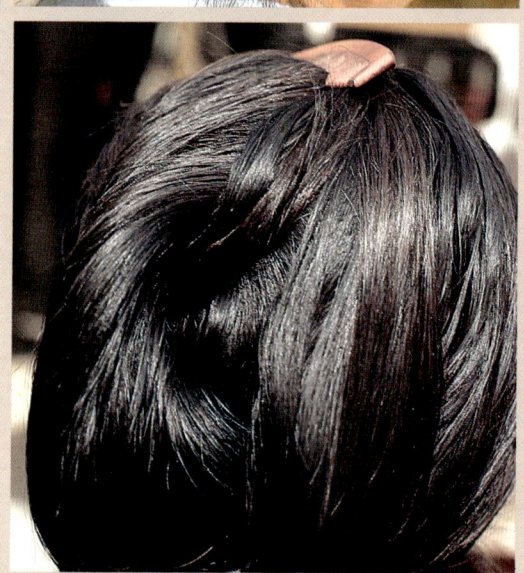

ORNAMENTS

Silver ornaments are another important aspect of a Dong woman's dress, especially among those in the south. Jewelry styles, though basically the same among the various Dong groups, do bear some distinctions such as the silver "weight" that hangs down the back of a woman's jacket (see page 65). This ornament, worn by many southern Dong women, holds the traditional backless under-apron in place. Several stories relate to the symbolism of wearing this distinct Dong ornament. Some say it is worn in remembrance of their ancestors, who, according to legend, were once held captive in ropes. Others hold the belief that by wearing this silver, they will avoid evil by thwarting malevolent spirits, thus ensuring a long life. Additionally, it is viewed as having both practical value and beauty, as well as a visual record of family wealth; a rich family's daughter would wear a much larger and heavier silver back ornament than a poor family's.

The back silver piece in some areas is formed in a shape known as the "mandarin duck pattern", which is considered an auspicious motif. This design (of two concentric circles oppositely joining) is also embroidered on baby carriers, and collars of women's jackets. In other Dong areas, the women wear heavy octagonal or square back silver pieces. These silver back ornaments are worn everyday, whether working in the fields or staying at home.

Above: Jewelry is made of silver or tin depending on a family's wealth.

Below: Children are often clothed in hats decorated with colorful embroidery and silver figurines.

From the time of childhood, silver ornaments are worn on hats, around wrists, necks and ears. During festivals, young unmarried women are richly adorned in a wide variety of silver jewelry: combs, hairpins, neckrings, earrings, necklaces, rings, pendants, headdresses, bells and bangles. All such jewelry is handcrafted by village silversmiths.

Above: Chengyang, Sanjiang Dong women wear heavy silver necklets during festive occasions. Jewelry forms vary from area to area.

Below: Embroidered under-apron yoke from Sanjiang worn with silver chain.

Above: Dong women from the south cherish the shiny effect of indigo-dyed cloth, steamed in eggwhites. Jacket sleeves made of this cloth are further beautified by embroidery. Heavy silver bracelets are worn by most women.

Below: A silver weight, worn by many southern Dong women, holds the traditional backless under-apron in place. Shapes vary according to region, though most are of the "mandarin duck" pattern.

ARCHITECTURE

Dominating the landscape of a Dong village is the drum tower with its superb formation of multi-storied pagoda-like roofs, constructed entirely without nails — a testimony to the unique architecture of the Dong nationality.

The lower pavilion of each tower is where villagers congregate during festivals and special meetings. People often gather there in the evenings, to listen to traditional folk songs. After harvests, young people hold festive dances on the grounds surrounding the drum tower.

The drum tower is the highest and most revered structure in the village. A giant drum within the tower served in the past as a warning device against invasions. In ancient times, villagers assembled at the tower with their weapons to await orders from the head of their clan.

Drum towers are a specialty and symbol of the Dong nationality. They first appeared in villages along the Yellow River during the Northern Dynasties (386-581 A.D.). The oldest standing drum towers date from the Shunzhi period (1644-1661 A.D.) of the Qing Dynasty.

A typical large village consists of from 500 to 600 families, and a small one, of about 50 families. As a rule, one village is said to contain families of one or two surnames. Each drum tower signifies one surname; some villages have two or three drum towers, therefore indicating that two or three surnames dominate the village.

Opposite: Drum Tower from Jitang village, Zhaoxing, Liping.

The outline of a Dong drum tower resembles a fir tree, a sacred tree in Dong culture. Some anthropologists have suggested that the Dong people used to be tree-dwellers, since they are believed to be a branch of the ancient Yue people, a tree-dwelling tribe.

Dong people visit neighboring villages during festivals to admire their towers. At such times, the villagers sing in praise of the tower's grandeur, pray for rich harvests, and wish their elderly longevity. Next to the elegant lines of the drum tower, they sing, dance and hold "lusheng" competitions.

Below: Painted floral designs decorate edgings of a drum tower.

Bottom: Carved figure of a lion makes its home on the roof of a Dong theatre.

Left: Dong homes, from two to three stories high, are likewise constructed without nails. The posts of a house are made of huge fir logs, notched to fit the connecting horizontal beams which are then secured by dowelling.

Opposite: The inside walls of a Dong covered bridge are painted with scenes from Dong and Han folk tales. Railings on the bridge offer additional space for villagers to hang their drying vegetables.

Above (right): Carved dragons "guarding a treasure", entwine through the railings above a gate tower entrance at Jitang, Zhaoxing.

Right: Hanging porch beams of Dong homes are often decoratively carved.

Below: Any available spot on the many-tiered eaves of drum towers are elaborately painted with scenes from old legends and folk stories, and embellished with statues of mythical creatures.

The "two dragons guarding a treasure" motif is a favorite of the Dong people and is often found on drum towers.

The insides and outer eaves of drum towers and covered bridges are often colorfully painted with scenes from Dong folk tales, legendary heroes, landscapes, animals and of activities such as ox-fighting and festive dancing. Aspects of daily life are likewise portrayed, such as playing musical instruments, hunting, spinning, weaving and dyeing, and the making of foods such as "baba". Carvings of dragons, snakes, tigers, geese, and occasionally even airplanes, ornament the roofs.

Above: Two of the five drum towers in Zhaoxing village.

Below: A Zhaoxing drum tower's octagonal roof is ornamented with three dragons guarding a treasure. The two figures below are about to compete with one another for obtaining the treasure.

Opposite: Village gate tower in Jitang, Zhaoxing

Covered wooden bridges, known among the Dong as "wind and rain" bridges, are another architectural landmark of Dong country that grace the area's many rivers and streams. Such bridges offer sheltered rest for weary travellers and protection from the elements. The Chengyang bridge is a famous horizontal-cantilever bridge of four spans over the Linxi River in Guangxi province. Each pier is crowned by pavilions of many-tiered roofs, linked by tiled roofs making the entire 64.6 meter bridge a covered walk. Not a single nail was used in its construction. It is bound together by mortise and tenon construction. Prior to 1906, no bridge spanned the flowing Linxi, creating many hardships for the Dong villagers during the high water seasons. In 1906 work began on the bridge after skilled architects from several nearby villages worked together drawing up plans. Eleven years later the bridge was complete.

"Wind and rain" bridges are a common sight throughout the southern Dong areas though those in Chengyang are among the largest. In other places such bridges span tiny meandering streams and are built primarily for their beauty and function as a social gathering spot on hot or rainy afternoons.

Below: The unique cultural landscape of the Dong generally includes covered bridges and drum towers. Beyond the famous Chengyang bridge stands the drum tower of Chengyang village, surrounded by China Fir, pine, Chinese tallow and Chinese larch. Bamboo water wheels, from one to four meters in diameter, are used for irrigating fields along the banks of the Linxi River.

Opposite: Cantilever bridge of two spans in Chengyang, Sanjiang.

Above: Carved details on eaves of drum tower portray images of the phoenix and dragon.

Below: The largest Dong drum tower stands in Mapang, Sanjiang.

Roof of drum tower ornamented with a clay lion.

Above and right: Details of Chengyang bridge

Preceding page: The village drum tower is always the site of important occasions, such as during the lunar New Year when thousands of villagers gather in the courtyard of the drum tower amid sounds of gongs and firecrackers for a songfest. Led by an old man, here the men join in singing traditional Dong folk songs in Chengyang, Sanjiang.

Above and left: Inside construction of drum tower.

About 20 meters high, Dong towers are made of fir, and secured with mortises and tenons instead of nails. The upper storeys feature a building technique called "dougong" where brackets are inserted at the intersections of columns and crossbeams. Each bracket consists of a double bow-shaped arm called a "gong" which supports a block of wood called a "dou". The roofs are square, hexagonal or octagonal.

Wood is cut from nearby forests, and is then hand sawn into lumber by the men of the village. As a rule, old trees in and near villages are considered inhabited by protective spirits. Such sacred trees must never be cut down. If this ever occurs, the one responsible must sacrifice an ox, and the wood can then only be used to construct a drum tower. Any remaining wood scraps must be used as fuel for inside the drum tower, not by an individual in his home.

Believing that the music of the lusheng if played during the rice-planting season leads to poor harvests, the Dong people block the holes of their lushengs and tie them to a pillar of the drum tower during this period.

Traditions are passed down orally and the drum towers become an important link in the process. All summer the drum towers offer the villagers cool water; in winter, a warm fire. After a day's work, people young and old gather there to reiterate ancestral legends, to narrate episodes of Dong history, or to teach traditionary folk songs and operas.

In the years to come, as modernization slips further and further into the mountains and valleys inhabited by the Dong, change is inevitable. Yet the Dong are a cohesive group with a strong cultural identity, and the current outward manifestations of their unique culture persist, especially in the south. Their distinct folk arts and customs, as representations of the Dong nationality and as mirrors of their ancestral history, will no doubt continue to develop and flourish in the forseeable future, adding to the richness of the world's folk ways.

Top: Endpost detail from a Dong theater house.

Above: Carved figure perches underneath eaves of a Dong theater.

Below: Painted designs embellish eave of a drum tower roof.

Preceding page: An elderly man sweeps the floor of the Chengyang bridge in the early morning sun.

Below: Dong mothers help dress their daughters in readiness for the New Year festivities.

ACKNOWLEDGEMENTS

We wholeheartedly thank the following people for their kindness and help during our many journeys throughout Guizhou, Guangxi and Hunan, enabling us to properly document this introduction to the Dong culture: Wang Chaowen (Governor of Guizhou), Long Chaoyun, Lu Genmao, Long Kailong, Dong Yaogang, Li Qianbin, Wu Zengou, Pan Jiarong, Wu Po, Wang Jun and Zhao Xuehai. Much gratitude to Dorothy Miller for her expertise concerning the information for spinning and warp preparations on pages 68-69 and likewise many thanks to Lisken Rossi for her help in translating numerous Chinese materials concerning the Dong people.

GAIL ROSSI

Born in 1951, Gail spent nine years in China (1980-1989) together with her husband Tony and three children. While Tony taught English to Chinese students in Beijing, Gail, a textile artist, spent her time researching the folk arts of China's nationalities. Concentrating on Guizhou Province, she explored remote mountainous areas inhabited by various nationalities, and documented the wide variety of folk arts and related customs, as well as ancient techniques employed to create traditional costume. Her experience of making 36 such journeys to Guizhou provided the background and inspiration to write over 20 articles on Guizhou's ethnic folk arts, and to curate the first exhibit of exclusively Guizhou minority textiles to tour North America. She is currently editing a series of books on China's folk arts, and together with her husband has organized a special foundation aimed to both help preserve China's unique folk arts and to assist rural education among China's ethnic nationalities.

PAUL LAU

Lau, born in 1959, has been a professional photographer based in Hong Kong since 1983. With his fluency in Mandarin and free access to all parts of China, he extensively travelled throughout the country to photograph landscape and people. Eventually, Lau focused his main attention on exploring the rugged and remote mountains of southwest China which are inhabited by numerous minority groups virtually unknown to the rest of the world. His special rapport with these rural poeple resulted in repeated visit in his attempt to visually record the customs, folk arts and traditional beauty of these little-known ethnic groups. He contributed as chief photographer for the book *The Forgotten Tribes of China*. His work appears in many international books and periodicals such as *China Unknown*, *China the Beautiful Cook Book,* and *GEO*. Lau was chosen as one of the photographers for the book project *China — The Long March*. He was also involved in the book titled *Over China*, working as a location consultant and as one of the principal photographers.

Dong girl in winter costume eating "baba".

THE DONG PEOPLE OF CHINA —
A HIDDEN CIVILIZATION

is designed and published by Hagley & Hoyle
Pte Ltd, Singapore

For book orders, please contact:
Hagley & Hoyle Pte Ltd,
70 Shenton Way #03-03
Marina House Singapore 0207.
Telephone: 2240688
Fax: 2246998

All rights reserved. No part of this publication may be
reproduced or used in any form or any means whether
graphical, electronic or mechanical, including
photocopying, recording, taping or information storage
and retrieval systems without the express written
permission of the publisher.

© Hagley & Hoyle Pte Ltd, Singapore
ISBN: 981-00-1551-8